MW01123889

TRIUMPHING OVER
LONELINESS

GREGORY DICKOW

Triumphing Over Loneliness:
The Influence of Connection
©2018 by Gregory Dickow Ministries.

All rights reserved.

No part of this book may be used or reproduced in any manner whatsoever—
graphic, electronic, or mechanical—without written permission, except in the case
of reprints in the context of reviews.

Printed in the United States of America

For information, please write:
Gregory Dickow Ministries
P.O. Box 7000
Chicago, IL 60680

You can visit us online at:
www.gregorydickow.com

ISBN 13: 978-1-932833-31-7

First Printing, 2018

TABLE OF CONTENTS

YOUR LOVE IS BETTER THAN WINE

Chapter One

Mother Teresa once said, "Loneliness and the feeling of being unwanted is the most terrible poverty." And if you've ever felt it, like most of us have, you know how right she was.

I heard someone say once: *"I thought marriage would bring me fulfillment and free me from loneliness; and so I prayed for a husband, while I waited for my life to start. Thankfully, God met me in my ignorance and showed me how wrong I was. He had better plans for me."*

This really struck me. I'm certainly not making an argument against marriage. Marriage was God's idea; but so was being a satisfied single! But, what really stood out to me were her words: *"while I waited for my life to start"*.

This book is all about not waiting for your life to start. It's time to start living and start enjoying the life God intended you to live. Loneliness is NOT your destiny. And loneliness is NOT what's going to define or confine you. Loneliness IS a signal. Its an invitation to intimacy with God.

"I've only been married six months" one woman wrote, *"but I feel completely alone—that I don't matter, like a puppy sitting under the table begging for scraps, looking for some sign that he still loves me. I know I am pathetic to need this, and hate it."*

What would make a woman feel so empty and worthless? It's that desperate craving for love, to fill the lonely place in the human heart.

We all have that craving. And Jesus has the answer!

". . . Because you are precious to me and because I love you and give you honor, do not be afraid—I am with you!" (Isaiah 43:4–5) The presence of God is the difference. And I'm believing that His manifest presence is going to fill you, heal you and flood your entire being from the inside out today!

But the devil wants to get you into a place of darkness and loneliness; *"to keep you trapped and hidden away with none to deliver . . . "* (Isaiah 42:22). His goal is to keep you lonely and isolated, so you will lose hope and quit.

But everything broken in your life, every bit of loneliness, disappointment, betrayal, or lack, is not a sentence to hope-lessness. Rather they are an INVITATION to intimacy with God, where you can never be disappointed. Loneliness is an invitation to reconnect with God in the deepest parts of your life.

"For your love is better than wine . . . the very mention of your name is like intoxicating oil." (Song of Solomon 1:2–3)

The Song of Solomon describes the relentless, passionate love that Jesus has for us, and how nothing can separate us from that love. The SONG OF SOLOMON IS ALL ABOUT JESUS AND YOU.

But Solomon was inspired by the Holy Spirit to write three books in the Bible: Proverbs, Ecclesiastes, and Song of Solomon.

These three books reflect the progression of our walk with God. **When we start our journey with Him, we begin in a place of illumination and awakening to the truth. This is our "Proverbs" experience. We feel settled, balanced, and fulfilled. We're full of understanding,** where most everything makes sense. **The book of Proverbs—the principles of life; cause & effect; wisdom vs. foolishness—gives us stability to stand secure in life.** Life is good and begins going the way we expect it to. But then, one day, it changes. We enter a season of confusion and disorientation. **We sense a loss of direction.** We feel disillusioned because of the trials and disappointments we experience. Life doesn't seem to be meeting our expectations. This is our "Ecclesiastes" season—*"Vanity of vanities."* (Ecclesiastes 1:2). The NIV says: *"Meaningless! Meaningless . . . Everything is meaningless."* The CEV translation says: *"Nothing makes sense. I have seen it all—nothing makes sense."* Pretty raw, right? Have you ever been through a season where nothing seems to make sense? The key to solving anything starts with being vulnerable and ruthlessly honest with ourselves, without giving up in those times when life feels meaningless and senseless.

It's amazing that Solomon went through these 3 seasons—these 3 books, so different, but all so profound.

Crazy isn't it? Can this 'vanity of vanities' guy be the same guy that wrote: *"Blessed is the one who finds wisdom, and the one who gets understanding; for the gain from her is better than silver and her profit better than gold."* (Proverbs 3:13–14).

Yes! Same writer. Same guy. Different season in his life.

This is Ecclesiasties. A season of disillusionment and

loneliness, where life without the fullness of God is empty, confusing and uncertain.

After a season of struggle, as we continue on our journey of faith, we realize life isn't about "me". It includes "me", but not about only lonely "me".

It's about Him and me! You could call this RECONNECTION or **REORIENTATION**. This is the "Song of Solomon"—a love relationship with God. This is a love story—and the ultimate purpose of our lives.

This is discovering or returning to your first love. That's when true fulfillment is discovered or restored. That's where I hope this book helps take you.

Are you in the "Ecclesiastes" season of your life? Where you feel disoriented or confused? Life doesn't seem to make sense? Or maybe you know someone who feels that way (wink, wink), and perhaps this will help you help them!

Or maybe you're in a season of "Proverbs", where you understand the principles of life—cause and effect; wisdom vs. foolishness, right vs. wrong. But that isn't as comforting as it once was.

I've found, as a believer now for over 30 years and a preacher for most of them, that life isn't always as black and white as we'd like it to be. Sometimes it's very gray. Yes, there is right and wrong. And I'm not trying to justify gray choices or ways of thinking. I've just come to a place where I've realized knowledge puffs up; but love builds up. (1 Corinthians 8:1) Just sheer knowledge of right and wrong will not satisfy you. It satisfies the self-righteous, but not the transparent, the self-aware, and the authentic person that wants the deeper meaningful walk with God—that we know in our heart of hearts God has called us to. And THAT'S who I believe you are!

The cure to loneliness is intimacy with God. This is what Solomon comes into the discovery of, as the Song of Solomon unfolds—the beauty of intimacy. In his crowning achievement, he finds his purpose, destiny and total fulfillment in life. Did he find it just in having wisdom? No. He had wisdom, but still came to a place of disillusionment. Did he find it in building the temple? No. He built the temple and still lost heart. Did he find it in relationships? Hahahahaha! The man had 700 wives and 300 concubines! Talk about a player! And he was still lonely.

No, none of those things were his crowning achievements. It was the revelation of the love that God revealed to him through the book of Song of Solomon—the story of love. Regardless of the exact timing of this book, God, in His infinite wisdom, had it placed after the other two books Solomon wrote.

God is showing us here: first we are enlightened, then, at times, disillusioned; but the season that heals it all is when we come to realize life is all about our marriage with Jesus!

Life without God in the center of it, is exactly what the enemy is after for our lives. It started in the garden.

Satan got Adam and Eve focused on themselves. THEY THOUGHT IT WAS ALL ABOUT THEM. They were wrong. They thought it was all about gaining knowledge. They were wrong. And that's when everything went wrong for them. That's when everything goes wrong for all of us.

Relationships and knowledge and fruit on trees can be great. But only when they are a complement, not a substitute for our intimacy with God.

Think of some of these great verses that prophetically speak of the beautiful relationship each of us are called into with Jesus Christ . . .

"Let him kiss me with the kisses of his mouth—for your love is more delightful than wine." (Song of Solomon 1:2)

"Let him lead me to the banquet hall, and let his banner over me be love." (Song of Solomon 2:4) I believe this speaks of the marriage of the Lamb. He's the groom and believers are the bride! That day is coming.

"Take me away with you—let us hurry! Let the king bring me into his chambers. We rejoice and delight in you; we will praise your love more than wine. How right they are to adore you!" (Song of Solomon 1:4)

"My beloved spoke and said to me, 'Arise, my darling, my beautiful one, come with me'." (Song of Solomon 2:10) The rapture? *"Come with Me!"*

There is so much more, but this is a glimpse of how Jesus feels about you.

Is there a lonely spot in your soul? It's not necessarily a bad thing. It's an invitation into the kind of intimacy these verses describe.

Jesus speaks to the heart of this intimacy and this calling to true fulfillment when He speaks to the church at Ephesus to return to their first love. (Revelation 2:4) He is our first love. And when we use anyone or anything else to fill the hole in our soul, we will eventually come up empty.

And so many people are doing just that.

THE GROWING EPIDEMIC OF LONELINESS

Chapter Two

A recent national survey exploring the impact of loneliness in the United States revealed that most American adults consider themselves lonely. The survey revealed some alarming findings:

- **Nearly half** of Americans report sometimes or always feeling alone or left out.

- **One in four** Americans rarely or never feel as though there are people who really understand them.

- **Almost half** of Americans sometimes or always feel that their relationships are not meaningful.

- **One in five** people report they rarely or never feel close to people or feel like there are people they can talk to.

- **Around half** of single parents/guardians—**even though they live with children, are more likely to be lonely.**

- **Generation Z (adults ages 18–22) is the loneliest generation** and claims to be in worse health than older generations.

What do these studies tell us? We've never lived in a more "connected" world, and yet with all the connection of technology, social media, etc., we've never been more DISCONNECTED and lonely. Now you may be in an amazingly healthy walk with God and other believers; but so many aren't, even many who are saved.

So lonely is this world that we look to others to fill our hearts with comfort and satisfaction. Many relationships are unhealthy because we are looking for people to satisfy a need only God can satisfy.

" . . . *He has also set eternity in the hearts of men.*" (Ecclesiastes 3:11)

You see, there is an eternal God-shaped hole in each of our hearts, and as much as we try to fill it with people and things, we still come up empty. Even good people and good things will leave us longing still, with a yearning that only God can satisfy. We were not created to be alone. We were created to be filled with Him and His love.

So often people are trying to fill that empty part of their life with friends, popularity, success, attention, or other people's accolades. And while no man is an island, and we need each other in healthy relationships, we have a God-shaped vacuum that can only be filled by God!

Aristotle said: *"No one would choose a lonely existence even if offered all the other things in the world. There were many that would rather meet their bitterest enemy in the field than to meet their own heart in the closet."*

People are lonely inside. They don't want to be by themselves. They don't want to face what it's like in that hole inside. But that hole is a signal. It's a signal that there's an eternal round peg that fits into that eternal round hole. It's Jesus.

Our world is filled with relationships, as is our lives, but many of these relationships are unhealthy because we're trying to get from each other what only God can give to us.

A table is made to stay intact under the weight of food, plates, glasses, and even elbows! But if you stand one or two or three people on the table, the stress placed upon it, will damage or break it.

So it also is with our relationships, whether it be our friends, our families, even our marriages—they are designed to hold the weight of light pressure and conflict (along with kindness and generosity). However, we are not designed to fill the hole of loneliness in the deepest place of each other's hearts. Only God can fill that hole. We are not designed to carry the burden of other people's happiness and fulfillment. When we allow the weight of those things to rest on us, in our relationships, the stress of those expectations damages or breaks our relationships and our hearts. That's one of the main reasons people have so much conflict, anger, and disappointment in their relationships.

CHANGE EXPECTATIONS BEFORE YOU CHANGE RELATIONSHIPS

Chapter Three

We need to adjust our expectations of people. We often have it backwards. We have an elevated expectation of people satisfying our emotional need and a low expectation on God satisfying it.

The irony is: only He can!

"It is better to trust in the LORD than to put confidence in man." (Psalm 118:8)

We get angry at people because they didn't give to us what we were expecting from them. But sometimes it's a blessing for a person to disappoint us or in some cases, even leave our lives! It's good because we were not designed to put our hope in them anyway.

I've had my heart broken, promises broken, and hopes shattered many times in over five decades on earth. And as painful as these seasons can be (as Ecclesiastes says, nothing makes sense), they are only seasons, not lifetimes, if we let it signal to us that God is drawing us into a more intimate love relationship with Him.

These breaks are not forever. Because nothing can permanently break an eternal heart. But the Lord can fill and heal a broken heart.

Though broken relationships bring pain in our lives, the redeeming grace of God causes our eyes to be opened to the depth of our need for a Savior.

I wonder if all of our moments of disappointment, disillusioned relationships, the bitter moments that may have scarred our lives, the offense, the mistreatment, failed marriages, or broken dreams could be turned into a massive awakening in our heart to run to the Refuge—our strong tower—the Lord—and lover of our soul.

"In you, LORD, I have taken refuge; let me never be put to shame; deliver me in your righteousness. Incline Your ear to me; come quickly to my rescue. Be my rock of refuge, the stronghold of my deliverance." (Psalm 31:1–2)

David was lonely when he wrote this. He was failing in strength. He cried out for a refuge. The word refuge means: a secret place of security and safety.

God is showing us here that the SECRET to the loneliness and disappointment we feel is the place of God's presence—where there is refuge, security, and safety.

David's broken relationships and adversaries woke him up to his need for God as His refuge.

"Among all my enemies I am a disgrace and among my neighbors all the more. I am dreaded by my friends—they flee when they see me on the street. I am forgotten like a dead man, out of mind. I am like a broken vessel." (Psalm 31:11–12)

But David didn't let adversity and pain sweep over his soul for long. He responds with the same faith YOU possess!

"But as for me, I trust in You, O LORD, I say, "You are my God." (Psalm 31:14)

"Let your favor shine on your servant. In your unfailing love, rescue me." (Psalm 31:16)

God's grace and unfailing love rescued him and will rescue you! It will rescue you from the pain others have caused. It will rescue you from the disappointment life has brought. It will rescue you from the disillusionment that this fallen world and human nature bring. It will rescue you from the loneliness that you may feel.

DISPELLING THE MYTH OF MAN'S LONELINESS

Chapter Four

Hi single, married or divorced person reading this right now! Oh, that's anyone reading this right now!

Marriage is NOT God's answer to loneliness.

How many times have we read the verse in Genesis and maybe got a little disappointed or hardened by the thought that this scripture wasn't a reality in our lives?

"Then the LORD God said, 'It is not good for the man to be alone; I will make him a helper suitable for him'." (Genesis 2:18)

Now I love the Word of God and I'll bet you do too! But some scriptures confound me sometimes, until the Holy Spirit gives revelation and we read it in context of the bigger picture of God's greater plan & purpose.

The scripture goes on to say:

"So the LORD God caused the man to fall into a deep sleep, and while he slept, He took one of the man's ribs and closed up the area with flesh. And from the rib that the LORD God had

taken from the man, He made a woman and brought her to him". (Genesis 2:21–22)

Beautiful scripture, right? Absolutely.

But the problem with our modern day application of the first creation of man, is that it sentences single people to a life of loneliness and incompleteness.

That cannot be what God is saying. If being married is the only way to be complete and the only way to satisfy the loneliness of the heart, then millions of people are damned in this life!

Being married can be great; but I know a lot of lonely husbands and wives. And being single can be great, but I know a lot of lonely single people.

On the other hand, I know (and so do you), many married people that are content; and many single people that are as well. But their contentment is not because of their marital status. It's because of an inward contentment that comes from the presence of God in that eternal hole. And their awareness of His presence is what satisfies them internally, making their status a content one, whether married, single, divorced, or widowed.

You see, it's God's eternal presence that fills the loneliness of the human heart.

Human marriage is NOT eternal. If it were, then Jesus would never have said:

"For in the resurrection they neither marry nor are given in marriage, but are like angels in heaven." (Matthew 22:30)

Now, if you're married, God certainly wants your relationship to be a piece of heaven on earth. And it can be very gratifying in many ways. But the truth is, marriage is a shadow, a picture of the ultimate marriage coming between us and Jesus, as we talked about earlier. That's the picture God paints in the Song of Solomon and in the book of Revelation.

"Let us rejoice and celebrate and give Him the glory. For the marriage of the Lamb has come, and His bride has made herself ready." (Revelation 19:7)

The answer to loneliness is not marriage. Nor is it playing the field and going from relationship to relationship. Using people to fill a hole in ourselves is actually pretty selfish. If we have a worldview that: "finding that perfect (or nearly perfect ☺)

one for me, will truly make me happy", all we're doing is objectifying the other person for our own gratification.

Now again, disclaimer: I'm not saying that your marriage can't be awesome. But remember my illustration about the table designed to hold certain things? But when asked to hold more weight than what it was designed for, it will break.

Our personal relationships are meant to complement our lives, not complete them.

So, if the answer to loneliness is NOT marriage, then what IS?

I'm glad you asked!

Remember the verse where it says: And from the side of man, God took a rib and fashioned it into a woman? And brought her to him? And I'm sure Eve was as hot and fine as you can imagine! (Nice gift to wake up to in the morning, right?!!!) God's good at what He does.

But the Bible talks about two creations. The first creation as described in Genesis. And then the NEW creation, which started at the cross, where Jesus shed His blood. 2 Corinthians 5:17 says, "If any man is in Christ, he is a new *creation; the old things are passed away and all things have become new."*

Check out this beautiful picture of God's love and how He completes us:

"But one of the soldiers pierced His side with a spear, and immediately blood and water came out." (John 19:34)

Notice the beautiful similarities between these two "creations".

In Genesis, because man was alone, God put Adam to sleep, and from his side, woman came forth to join Adam to fulfill their destiny.

In the Gospel, because man was alone without hope and without God, God put Jesus to sleep, (through the cross), and Jesus was pierced in His side and the Bride was born to join Jesus in His destiny!

Through His blood, we were born! Through His water, our minds are renewed and we are filled with the living water of the Holy Spirit!

"This is the One who came by water and blood, Jesus Christ; not with the water only, but with the water and with the

blood. *It is the Spirit who testifies, because the Spirit is the truth.*" (1 John 5:6)

You see? The Holy Spirit is the New Creation Helper!

That doesn't mean that women don't help. They sure the heck do! They're the best. But now, women are the same "new creation" in Christ that men are! In Christ, we are not defined by male and female, but as equal sons and daughters of God.

And the Holy Spirit comes to be our Helper—not coming from the inside, to live next to us; but coming from the outside to live INSIDE of us.

THE ANSWER IS THE HOLY SPIRIT

Chapter Five

"Nevertheless, I tell you the truth: it is to your advantage that I go away, for if I do not go away, the Helper will not come to you. But if I go, I will send him to you." (John 16:7)

In the first creation, God took the helper out from within Man. In the new creation, God puts the Helper IN MAN.

He comes to help us from within. This completes us, satisfies us, and gives us purpose in our lives.

Whether single, married, divorced, or struggling in any way, He is the answer! He is the answer to a lonely man, woman, or child. And He is also the answer to a lonely marriage. He can make the difference, as both people seek His inner contentment and help.

I love how Jesus describes the "help" that the Holy Spirit brings in our lives in the Amplified version of this verse:

*"But I tell you the truth, it is to your advantage that I go away; for if I do not go away, the **Helper (Comforter, Advocate,***

Intercessor—Counselor, Strengthener, Standby) will not come to you; but if I go, I will send Him (the Holy Spirit) to you [to be in close fellowship with you]." (John 16:7, AMPC)

Notice the 7 things the Holy Spirit will do in your life:

(1) Helper, (2) Comforter, (3) Advocate (Defender), (4) Intercessor, (5) Counselor, (6) Strengthener, (7) Standby.

He helps us to know what to do. He helps us with encouragement. He helps our weaknesses. He helps us pray. He helps in every way.

With all this help, who could stay lonely, discouraged or disappointed?!!!

Jesus did not live His life, perform His miracles, preach His sermons, nor do His works as God. He did them as a Spirit-filled man. Luke 4:1 says, *"And Jesus being full of the Holy Spirit returned from Jordan, and was led by the Spirit into the wilderness."* That same Holy Spirit has been made available to every Christian so that every one in the world will have an opportunity to see the amazing life that Jesus lived. Now every country can see Him, every business can see Him, every neighborhood can see Him, and every school can see Him.

Have you tried and failed like me? Have you ever found that you would rather be served than serve, that you would rather be helped than to help? Have you found that you would rather hate your enemies than love them?

Have you tried to live holy and failed; to share your faith, and struggled? To overcome a habit or addiction, but just couldn't get it turned around? Tried to turn a little into a lot; but it seems whenever you have a lot, it turns into a little?

As hard as we've all tried, we've failed. We could not be like Him—**in our own power that is. That's another reason God gave us the Holy Spirit—to transform our lives**. In Romans 8:11, it says, *"But if the Spirit of Him that raised up Jesus from the dead dwells in you, He that raised up Christ from the dead shall also give life to your mortal bodies by His Spirit that dwells in you."*

Romans 8:11 is not talking about our coming physical resurrected body, but rather the availability of the resurrected life while we are yet in our present body. God is saying that if the Holy Spirit can raise up Jesus from the dead, that same Holy Spirit can raise you up from defeat & despair; loneliness & pain in order that you may live a resurrected life now. That resurrected life can be lived only in the power of the Holy Spirit.

Now suppose for a minute your child's greatest desire was to be a basketball player, yet he lacked the talent, skill, or size. (the trifecta of sure defeat ☺) You could take him to basketball camps and to little leagues, and maybe even a camp hosted by an NBA player, like Lebron James or Kevin Durant, Steph Curry or let's say . . . Michael Jordan in his prime . . .

No matter how many classes your child goes to, no matter how much mentoring your child could get from these great, current, and former NBA Hall of Famers, your child could not be like Mike, Lebron, Kevin or Steph. But if there was a way to unzip your child and have one of these players live inside of him, then he could!

That's why the Holy Spirit doesn't come to live BY us, or near us to coach us or mentor us; BUT IN US. (Romans 8:11, Galatians 4:6, 1 John 2:27, Ezekiel 36:27)

There is so much to say about this, but I want to share briefly with you how to activate the Helper, and the Help of the Holy Spirit. If you're born again, He lives in you. Here are some ways to activate His power:

By speaking God's Word. "*While Peter was speaking these words, the Holy Spirit fell on those who were listening.*" (Acts 10:44)

By asking Him to fill you. *" . . . How much more will your heavenly Father give the Holy Spirit to those who ask Him."* **(Luke 11:13)**

By praying in tongues. The Spirit helps our weaknesses when we pray with groanings too deep for words. (Romans 8:26, 1 Corinthians 14:14)

By worshiping Jesus. As they worshiped and glorified God, the glory of God filled the temple. (2 Chronicles 5:13–14)

Now, remember the difference between the help and glory of the old creation vs. the help and glory of the new creation.

Under the old covenant, the glory and help of God came DOWN from heaven or came from the outside.

In the new covenant, the glory comes OUT from within us!

Speak God's Word. Speak His praise. Worship in your heavenly language, and the Comforter, Encourager, and Strengthener will manifest in your life and through your life!

LOVE HEALS

Chapter Six

"Your love is better than wine." (Song of Solomon 1:2)

As I shared with you in the opening chapter, Mother Teresa said, *"Loneliness and the feeling of being unwanted is the most terrible poverty."*

How many of us have felt this loneliness or love deficit? **Perhaps you've felt the absence of love, but pushed it down or learned to tolerate it.** That can be the loneliest place of all.

The devil wants to get you into a place of darkness and keep you there so you will lose hope and quit.

But everything broken in your life, every disappointment, betrayal, lack, and loneliness, is an INVITATION to reconnect with God in that area of your life.

The love of God is the cure for loneliness. Because it fills the gaps and fills all the holes life and people have brought us. Consider the following verse—an amazing fulfillment of the promise to fill us to all of God's fullness.

"Now hope does not disappoint, because the love of God has been poured out within our hearts through the Holy Spirit who was given to us." (Romans 5:5)

It is the presence of God's love in our heart that delivers us from disappointment and the hopelessness that comes from loneliness.

It is the presence of the Holy Spirit that fills the eternity in our hearts—the eternal hole—with His irreversible presence!

Love Heals.

And Jesus, moved with compassion, healed their sick . . .

Moved with compassion, He fed the multitudes.

Moved with compassion, He touched the coffin and raised the boy from the dead.

The Love of God heals us of all emptiness, loneliness, and disappointment.

Some years ago, Dr. Karl Menninger, noted doctor and psychologist, was seeking the cause of many of his patients' ailments. One day he called in his clinical staff and proceeded to unfold a plan for developing, in his clinic, an atmosphere of creative love. All patients were to be given large quantities of love; no unloving attitudes were to be displayed in the presence of the patients, and all nurses and doctors were to go about their work in and out of the various rooms with a loving attitude. At the end of six months, the average time spent by patients in the institution was cut in half.

How was that possible? Because love never fails! It fills the holes and gaps in our lives. And because God is love, His healing power flows through that love.

THE MINISTRY OF THE HOLY SPIRIT

Chapter Seven

"To proclaim the day of vengeance of our God; to comfort all who mourn, to console those who mourn in Zion, to give them beauty for ashes, the oil of joy for mourning, the garment of praise for the spirit of heaviness; that they may be called trees of righteousness, the planting of the LORD, that He may be glorified." And they shall rebuild the old ruins, they shall raise up the former desolations . . ." (Isaiah 61:2–4)

The Holy Spirit came to bring the Day of Vengeance. And vengeance is not revenge.

Notice how He describes vengeance. He avenges us by turning our ashes into beauty. He avenges us by giving us the anointing and joy for grief and mourning. He avenges us by giving us a garment of praise for the spirit of heaviness.

Then He encourages, strengthens, and comforts us by calling us oaks of righteousness. He calls us that before we ever did any acts of righteousness. How great is He? I'll tell you how great He is: "Greater is He that is in you than he that is in the world!" (1 John 4:4)

He says in verse 3, that they might be called (or become something). He's saying that the Holy Spirit calls us what God says we are! He calls us everything that Jesus is.

Jesus said, "But the Helper, the Holy Spirit, whom the Father will send in my name, he will teach you all things and bring to your remembrance all that I have said to you." (John 14:26).

Without the Holy Spirit's presence in our lives, we wouldn't be able to be everything God says we are—because He is God in us and it is He who makes us one with God. His "calling" is not a vocation. It's what He calls us as sons and daughters; joint heirs with Him; the head and not the tail; blessed coming in and blessed going out. There are so many more things that the Holy Spirit calls us and comforts us with. And He lives IN us.

This is the cure to all loneliness: the presence of the Holy Spirit in our lives! He could have chosen to live anywhere in the universe or stayed in heaven. But He chose to live inside of you and me, the moment we are born again!

"Do you not know that you are a temple of God and that the Spirit of God dwells in you?" (1 Corinthians 3:16)

I believe one of the reasons people are lonely and seek so many other ways to fill that loneliness is because they don't KNOW that the Holy Spirit lives in them. They may have heard it. They may even think He comes and goes as they are obedient to Him. But that's not accurate. He lives in you, no matter what.

" . . . For He has said, *'I will never [under any circumstances] desert you [nor give you up nor leave you without support, nor will I in any degree leave you helpless], nor will I forsake or let you down or relax My hold on you [assuredly not]!' So we take comfort and are encouraged and confidently say, 'The Lord is my Helper [in time of need], I will not be afraid. What will man do to me?'"* (Hebrews 13:5–6, AMPC)

What can man do to you? No matter how many have left you, hurt you, disappointed you, abused you, and failed you, IT CAN'T HURT YOU forever. It CAN awaken you though to the reality that the Holy Spirit is your Helper!

He will never:

Desert you.

Give you up.

Leave you without support.

Leave you helpless.

Forsake you.

Let you down.

Relax His hold on you.

This is why it says we can take comfort and be encouraged! This is why we can boldly say, "*The Lord is my helper. I will not be afraid. What can man do to me?*"

Wow! Peace, freedom and fulfillment come from knowing He is with you and IN YOU!

It is time for every hole, every bruised or damaged area of your life, and every abused area of your life to be comforted. We think we need a friend or therapist to do what He wants to do within us—to comfort and heal, to restore what has been bruised, and to heal it. Nothing wrong with friends and therapists. But this is an inside job in the deepest places that man can't get to.

He does it with the Word. As you hear God's Word and speak His Word, the Holy Spirit releases the love that fills you, and the spiritual "power tools" to heal you. The Comforter heals, transforms and restores what's been empty, bruised, or damaged.

HE RESTORES MY SOUL

Chapter Eight

As a pastor and a teacher, my objective is not to focus on changing a person's behavior, because that's just behavioral modification. But my goal is to help you renew your mind so that you have right thinking and right believing. Then a *right-thinking* person will be a *right-living* person. A *right-believing* person will be a *right-living* person. So, my goal is not to try to tell you all the right things to do in your life, but to teach you the Word of God concerning how to think and believe, and that will produce victorious, enjoyable, and powerful living. That is God's will for each of us here on this earth. And that's why the Bible says in 2 Timothy 1:7, *"God has not given you a spirit of fear, but of power and of love and of a sound mind."*

What does it mean to have a sound mind? It means you have a healed mind, which means healed *emotions.* Sick emotions create sick lives, choices, and actions. This is why there is so much crime in the world: hate, murder, violence, and anger. Sick thinking produces sick living. When you think right, you begin to think healthy. It means you feel healthy, live healthy, and make healthy choices.

The soul is three things. The soul is the mind to think, the heart to feel, and the power or will to choose. And there is no greater gift that has been given to man by God (besides the gift of salvation), than the gift of choice—the gift to be able to choose the outcome of our life. Remember the 90/10 rule: life is 10% of what is done to us, but 90% of what we choose—how we choose to respond to what's been done to us.

In the next chapter, I want to share with you about how God goes about healing the soul that's broken. Get ready to receive supernatural healing for your soul—God's way!

HEALING THE LONELINESS THAT COMES FROM A BROKEN SOUL

Chapter Nine

Now that we understand a little bit better about what our soul is and why it is broken or lonely, let's look at a real-life example of someone in the Bible who had a broken soul, and see how Jesus brought healing and deliverance to him. In Luke 8:27, it says,

"When Jesus stepped out on the land, there met him a man from the city who had demons for a long time."

I want you to notice that the devil loves to keep people in bondage for a **long time**, but Jesus loves to set people free!

Look what the Bible says next.

" . . . and he wore no clothes, nor did he live in a house, but he lived in the tombs."

A damaged soul affects our financial condition, our living condition, and our relationships. So this miracle is going to affect all three areas of his life. This miracle also demonstrates

Jesus' dominion over the devil. And if Jesus has dominion over the devil, so do you! Jesus said in Luke 10:19, *"Behold, I give you the authority to trample upon serpents and scorpions, and over all the power of the enemy, and nothing shall by any means injure you, or hurt you."*

We've been pushed around by the devil for far too long. We've been given more authority than he has. But he has deceived us into thinking that he has more authority than we have. But God wants us to know that we have more authority than the devil has. We just need to learn how to walk in this authority, so that nothing shall by any means hurt us.

According to Romans 5:17, God has given us authority through the abundance of grace and the gift of righteousness. We reign in life! So, if we're not reigning in life, it's because we don't understand the abundance of grace, and we don't understand the gift of righteousness. So, where there is an absence of understanding grace and an absence of understanding the gift of righteousness, there will be an absence of victory. But where there is an abundance of grace and where there is an understanding of the gift of righteousness, there will be an abundance of victory and reigning in life.

Now I know there are people, even preachers out there that say, "Well sometimes God heals and delivers; and sometimes He doesn't." But you're smarter than that. You're smart enough to believe the Bible more than a preacher. The Word of God explains itself. We live in a fallen world. There's a real devil. People make bad decisions. We wreck our lives. We grow up being abused. We grow up with bad parenting. Sometimes we grow up making bad choices. We grow up and something is done to us that hurts us. We grew up with a DNA of some sort of sin. Some people grow up, and they're really susceptible to alcohol addiction. Other people are really susceptible to pornography. And other people are really susceptible to some opioid or some drug. Other people are really susceptible to craving everybody's attention and affection. And some of us, like me ☺ ended up growing up with all of those things—an all-in-one! He said, "Let me get this guy. Because if I get this guy saved, delivered, and healed, then it will be a picture of what God can do in anybody's life." I like to say, when God saved me, He saved the worst first!

Now, take a look at Matthew 8:16: *"That evening they brought to Him many who were oppressed by demons, and he cast out the spirits with a word and healed all who were sick."* This scripture shows Jesus' compassion for oppressed people, His commitment to see His finished work in you, and His fearlessness of Satan and anything Satan can do. Let's see what else we can find out about how God heals us from loneliness by healing the soul.

JESUS LOVES TO SET PEOPLE FREE

Chapter Ten

When we look at this demon-possessed man back in Luke 8:27, we, yet again, see Jesus' compassion for a lonely oppressed person. You're going to see His commitment to see His finished work in you, because He never leaves unfinished business in your life.

"As Jesus was climbing out of the boat, a man who was possessed (controlled) by demons came out to meet Him . . . " (Luke 8:27)

How does this deliverance apply to us? You may not be controlled by demons; but demonic thinking controls many people, even if the devil doesn't live inside of them. Because when you're born again, the Holy Spirit lives inside of you, but the Holy Spirit doesn't live in your thinking. You have to take control of your thinking.

The devil tries to influence us through the way we think; our mind-sets that are contrary to the Word of God. And its up to us to dispossess him by filling our thought life with God's way of thinking. As we do that, it leaves no room for the devil. This is resisting the devil (James 4:7). As you flood your mind with God's Word, the devil has to go. He can only ride on the saddle of wrong thinking in your life. As soon as you change the saddle and put God's way of thinking in your mind, then Satan can't ride that horse anymore! He's got to get off and get out of town, because this town ain't big enough for the both of us!

But . . . back to our story . . . Let's see what happens next:

"When he saw Jesus, he cried out, fell down before Him, and with a loud voice said, 'What have I to do with You, Jesus, Son of the Most High God? I beg You, do not torment me!'" (Luke 8:28, NKJV)

This is one of my favorite scriptures. Because when he saw Jesus, he fell down before Him and begged Him not to torment him. Now, the torment he's speaking of here is the eternal torment that the demons will experience in Hell. But it also speaks to me about religious-thinking people. **They think God is tormenting them.** But it's really the devil. Why would Jesus torment him? The only reason people think God intends them harm or leaves them in a broken or lonely condition is because they have a wrong view of God.

When you meet *the real Jesus*, the thought that He could torment you will never cross your mind. The thought that He would put sickness or disease or trouble in your life will never cross your mind when you meet the real Jesus. Everywhere He went, He lifted burdens. Everywhere He went, He loved the unlovable. Everywhere He went, He fed the hungry, had mercy on the sinner and compassion on the suffering. Everywhere He went, He healed the sick, raised the dead, cleansed the lepers and cast out demons. The only people He tormented were the religious people that thought they could be right with God through their own actions and through their own self-righteousness. He tormented their religion because their religion tormented people! And Jesus loves to set people free!

FREEDOM FROM LONELINESS AND SOLITARY PLACES

Chapter Eleven

Back to our story—Jesus continues to bring healing to this man—healing him from loneliness and oppression. Let's look at Luke 8:29:

"For He had commanded the unclean spirit to come out of the man. For it had often seized him, and he was kept under guard, bound with chains and shackles; and he broke the bonds and was driven by the demon into the wilderness." (Luke 8:29, NKJV)

In the New International Version (NIV) of Luke 8:29, the last part of the verse says, ***"he was driven by the demon into solitary places."*** Now, this is very relevant to our world today, because this reveals how Satan operates in people's lives and where violent people are conceived. I want you to see where terrorism is born and where violent crimes and murder originate. ***They originate from the devil driving people into a solitary place, a place of isolation.***

A solitary place represents a place where you're isolated from God, from love, from church, from family. You're isolated from people that will speak the truth to you in love. When we isolate ourselves, we become fertile soil for the seeds of loneliness, even violence—fertile soil for the seeds of hatred.

This is what happens in solitary places. Satan is trying to drive people to solitary places because that's where they remain abused. That's where they remain bruised by how they grew up. That's where they remain lonely. That's where they become loners. That's where they become people that have no other voices to challenge the voices in their head that are telling them to hurt themselves or someone else. It's in the "solitary places" that Satan is trying to drive people to. That's why the Bible says, *"God sets the solitary in families: he bringeth out those which are bound with chains . . . "* (Psalm 68:6).

That's why God puts people in healthy churches. We need the family of God, because Satan's trying to drive us into solitary places, where we're isolated from getting the help that we need.

Perhaps you have a friend or a loved one who's been given over to an addiction or some form of self-injury, or some emotion or mistake that has just overtaken them. When that happens, it's usually because, first that person was driven to a solitary place—a lonely place in their soul. They've withdrawn and retreated. And every person who does one of the heinous crimes we've seen displayed too many times, are usually loners who have been driven to a solitary place by the enemy of their soul.

That's the first place where we can practically walk in love and spiritual warfare—not just by binding the devil over their life, but by saying 'hi' to them. Greet the loner. I was a loner in school. I was a loner in junior high and in high school. I was withdrawn and depressed. By the age of 16 years old, I was addicted to drugs; I was an alcoholic. All of those things, I believe, came from an emotional place of isolation. I could have become one of those lone-wolf attackers or violent extremist killers. I could have become that because I was in a solitary place in my soul. I wasn't someone who would share what I was going through; I wouldn't let anybody in. I was guarded, invulnerable; I had a hidden life inside. My soul was in bondage, and I was afraid to let anybody into that soul that was so damaged, so afraid, so depressed, and discouraged. So, I guarded it. I protected it with external things. What I am trying to get across is that the best thing that ever happened to me was somebody busted through that solitary confinement that I was in and said, "Hey man, how you doing? Want to come to a Bible study with me?"

Somebody cared. Somebody reached out. Who knows what I would have become two years later if nobody would have reached out to me. I'm not saying that we're the reason why people do crazy things. But what I'm saying is: our love, our compassion, our reaching out to that loner, that person in our world and in our environment, the person at work, the person in your family, or the person in your neighborhood can make a difference. And don't be afraid. Love never fails. The love will break down walls and break down barriers, and love will cast out fear, and love will drive the fear out of their life and yours. And who knows what could happen?

But we know what happens when one is left to themselves in a solitary place. They're overcome by the devil. That's why the Bible says one can put a thousand to flight, and two can put 10,000 to flight. That's why the Bible says when you're planted in the house of God that's when you flourish. That's why the Bible says two are better than one because two can receive a better return for their labor, and a three-strand cord is not easily broken. That's why the Bible says where two or three are gathered in My name there I am in the midst of them. That's why the Bible says, if two of you shall agree about anything they ask it shall be done by my Father who's in heaven. There is deliverance, there is freedom, and there is a healing that comes to the soul through the power of connection—right connection that is.

Self-Injury

Let's look at Mark's version of this of this experience of the demon-possessed man. In Mark 5:5, it says, *"and always, night and day, he was in the mountains and in the tombs, crying out and cutting himself with stones."* Think about what he was doing. This is called self-injury. We think that this self-injury, people cutting themselves, and kids harming themselves is new and recent in the last 20–30 years. But this goes all the way back at least 2000 years. This guy was cutting himself. He was doing what so many people do at the youngest ages.

A recent study conducted at Princeton found that 17% of college students self-injured themselves. They cut, carve, burn, or otherwise hurt themselves. More recent data indicates that about 25% of adolescents have self-injured. That's one out of every four who are deliberately hurting themselves! A study revealed just a few years ago, showed 10% of third graders self-injured themselves and 15% of ninth graders cut themselves. They are trying to let out their pain; they don't know how else to do it. Each year, one out of five women and one out of seven men engage in self-injury, and that does not even scratch the surface of all the disorders—psychological, mental, or emotional disorders that people have.

I'm not trying to depress you with these statistics, but to make you aware of the world we live in today. This affects all of us because it affects your husband, or your wife, somebody you care about, or somebody close to you. Or it affects you! And you're suffering in silence. I want you to experience healing in your soul.

Eating disorders affect eight million people in America. Heroin addiction among 18 to 25 year olds has doubled in 10 years. Twenty-two veterans commit suicide in America every day. They're under so much post-traumatic stress disorder. They're under so much pain from what they've gone through or what they've done. God wants to heal them. Forty million people in America today suffer from anxiety. Three hundred and fifty million people worldwide suffer from depression today. Over 60 to 70 million people in America suffer from a health disorder. That's one out of every four adults, not including children. Almost 1 million people commit suicide each year. Around the world, 20 million people are dealing with substance abuse in America. One out of four women are suffering from domestic violence. Youths are suffering from violent deaths. 16 to 22 year olds are dying through violent deaths—10 times more in America than any other industrialized nation.

And this man who was self-injuring and trying to self-medicate himself is a picture of us. We can find ourselves here. Even though we don't have thousands of demons living inside of us, we have thousands of knives in our soul from what life has done to us. And I'm not trying to say that to make you a victim. I'm trying to say that to get you healed. And we need to let the world know there's a place they can come and find healing. There's a place they can come and find deliverance. There's a Person and a place they can come to and be delivered from the power of the devil and the power of the demonic mind-sets that have damaged people's lives. Jesus is that Person. The healthy church is that place. Most people are not dealing with a demon; they're dealing with the imprint that the demon has left in their mind. This guy was cutting himself. He was depressed. He was detached. And he was diseased. And this is the condition of people's souls. People's souls are depressed. Their souls are detached.

Now, these numbers that I gave you—those are only the numbers that are reported. And there are a lot of people that are dealing with depression, anxiety, eating disorders, and other things, but they don't report it. These statistics are based on the people that have admitted it. It doesn't even count all the people that hide it, all the people that are not letting us know, and all the people that may be silently suffering some sort of violent situation.

This is how we can help stop the violence in the world. **This is how we could change the world.** We have to look at the people around us and realize every one of us has a circle of influence with people we come in contact with. It may be that nobody else will come in contact with that hurting person in your life. Go hit that person up with some good old-fashioned kindness and love. You don't have to be their best friend over-night, but just shake their hand. Say, "How you doing?" or "Hey man it's going to be all right. Let me pray for you. If you ever need anything here's my number." This is one way God brings healing to our souls. Let's see how else we can receive healing for our soul.

CLOTHED AND IN YOUR RIGHT MIND

Chapter Twelve

Let's continue to watch this man's healing unfold. In Luke 8:30, the first thing Jesus says to the man is, *"What is your name?"* The man replies, "Legion". He has at least 6,000 demons living inside of him. He answered honestly, Legion, because many demons had entered him. **We have to name the thing that we're struggling with. Name it.** Why do you have to name it? Because only when you admit it, can Jesus deliver you from it. When something has a name, then the Name above all names will deliver you from that name.

When you name it, you're being honest about it. When you name it, you're inviting Jesus to deliver you from it and to heal you from it. When we're not honest about our struggle, we can't get delivered from it. When we hide it, we keep it. We keep it hidden, and it stays there; and it defeats us from within. So, call it out. When you refuse to admit a weakness or pretend that you're not dealing with it, it gets a stronger hold in your life. It operates in the "solitary places".

*"Then Jesus permitted the demons to go out of the man and enter the swine, and the herd ran violently down the steep place into the lake and drowned. When those who fed them saw what had happened . . . they came to Jesus, and found the man from whom the demons had departed, **sitting at the feet of Jesus, clothed and in his right mind . . ."*** (Luke 8:31–36, NKJV)

Notice, when they came to Jesus, they found the man from whom the demons had departed. And what was the man's condition? **He was sitting at the feet of Jesus, clothed and in his right mind;** but they were afraid. When the man was living among the dead, when he was breaking chains, when he was cutting himself with stones, when he was gnashing his teeth, and when he was crying out, yelling, and screaming, nobody was afraid. Now the man is sitting at the feet of Jesus—clothed, in his right mind—and people are freaking out! We have to stop getting used to things being abnormal!

When I was lonely and addicted, none of my friends or family members seemed too concerned. But after I got saved, they asked, "What's wrong with Greg?" Ha! Now I'm not doing drugs anymore. Now I'm not selling anymore. "What happened to him? We need to get him some help." You didn't need to get me help when I was addicted to drugs, but now Jesus found me and I'm free, and NOW you want to get me help? Haha! But thank God, Jesus is my Helper, and that is where my help comes from. Praise God! I'm just glad Jesus saved me and He's still working on me too. (Aren't you glad about that?☺)

Now notice, " . . . they came to Jesus, and found the man from whom the demons had departed, **sitting at the feet of Jesus, clothed and in his right mind . . ."**

I want to tell you what it means to be in your right mind. Follow the same pattern and you will be in your right mind and healed in your soul. When a man is in his right mind, he will worship the right thing. What do we find this man doing? Sitting and worshipping at the feet of Jesus, listening to His word, and renewing His mind. *The thing that will heal your soul is worshipping the right thing.* We worship so many wrong things. We worship people. We worship money. We worship ourselves. We worship people's opinion. We worship the number of likes on our Facebook or Instagram posts. But when you worship Jesus, you will be healed in your soul. The first thing he did: he worshipped the right thing.

The second thing he did was he associated with the right people. What does it say? He was found at the feet of Jesus. And then he begged Jesus, in Luke 8:38, to let him follow Him. The power of right associations will help heal you of loneliness and help you get in your right mind. This is why it's so important that you don't surround yourself with negative people, gossipers, negative mind-sets, people that are haters, complainers, and whiners. Surround yourself with the right people.

What healed his soul was that he worshiped the right thing. That is, Jesus. What healed his soul is he chose the right associations. That's Jesus and His disciples. The third thing is he wanted to follow Jesus everywhere He went.

"Now the man from whom the demons had departed begged Him that he might be with Him. But Jesus sent him away, saying, 'Return to your own house, and tell what great things God has done for you.' And he went his way and proclaimed throughout the whole city what great things Jesus had done for him." (Luke 8:38–39)

Jesus said: Go to your own house and tell them the great things God has done for you. ***The third thing that healed his*** *soul is right priorities. It starts in our own house.* That's where we learn to live out what God has put inside us.

It starts at home. Take God's Word home with you. That's how we get our priorities right. What we learn in the House of God is what we're called to live out in our own house.

And then it says, he went and told everybody about the great things that God had done. *He had the right praise.* Praise what God has done. Talk about the great things God has done in your life. Give Him thanks even for the littlest things—food on your table, clothes on your back, the air you get to breathe. AN attitude of praise and thankfulness for the goodness and grace of God will do your soul good! This is what heals you. **Worship the right thing.** That will help heal your soul. **Choose the right associations.** That will heal your soul. **Start walking in the right priorities.** Take what you're hearing and live it out at home. That'll heal your soul. **And choose the right praise.** What do you praise? *He praised God. He told of the great things God had done.* He lost interest in talking about all that people had done to him and he started talking about all that God had done for him.

Follow this pattern, and you will receive healing in your soul and never be lonely another day in your life!

A FINAL NAIL IN THE COFFIN OF LONELINESS

Chapter Thirteen

Everyone knows what it's like to feel lonely, depressed and afraid. The pressure against our emotions can be overwhelming at times. Who hasn't felt the waves of darkness try to take over their soul? I think we've all felt that at times. The devil wants to get you into a place of darkness and keep you there so you will lose hope and quit. The truth is that Jesus has destroyed the works of the devil (1 John 3:8), but we lose sight of that at times.

So what the enemy tries to do is paint a hopeless, dark picture of your life so you become discouraged, lonely, and depressed. You may be in a place like that right now. Or perhaps you know someone that is in that place.

So how do we break free from that place of loneliness and darkness? Psalm 119:30 says, *"The entrance of His Word brings light."* As we flood the light of God's Word into our heart, darkness, loneliness, & depression flee! David sure knew what it was like to go through these times:

"The enemy pursues me; he crushes me to the ground; he makes me dwell in the darkness like those long dead. So my spirit grows faint within me; my heart within me is dismayed." (Psalm 143:3–4)

But notice, as this darkness sweeps over his soul and overwhelms him, he remembers the Word of God. Let's look at how he breaks free from this loneliness & darkness: In fact, here are seven simple steps out of loneliness, depression, even discouragement, based on Psalm 143.

1. *"I remember the days of long ago; I meditate on all your works and consider what your hands have done."* (Verse 5) **Remember what God has done.** Deliberately go back and look at what God has already done for those in the Bible, and deliberately go back and look at what God has done in your life. This will bring comfort and encouragement to you. So much of why we feel what we feel is because of our memory. Bad memories meditated on, produce dark lonely emotions. Good memories meditated on produce encouraging, joy-filled emotions.

2. *"I spread out my hands to you."* (Verse 6) **This is all about worship.**

No matter what it feels like, the way out of darkness and loneliness is to put on praise. You can't worship God and stay lonely at the same time. The presence of God is not something we have to strive and struggle to enter into. We enter into His presence by the blood of Jesus. (Hebrews 10:19)

As you lift your hands and voice to God in thanks and adoration, your mind and heart will feel lifted too. Worship Him because He IS so good; even when things don't look so good.

3. *"Answer me speedily."* (Verse 7) **Listen for and expect God to answer the cry of your heart. Remember, we can ALWAYS go to the throne of grace to receive mercy and grace in our time of need.** Expect to hear an answer; expect a door to open.

4. *"Let the morning bring me word of your unfailing love, for I have put my trust in you."* (Verse 8) **Greet your day meditating on God's love for you.** This sets the course of your day.

The greatest happiness in life is the assurance that we are loved. Find one verse each day about God's love, until it drives out all fear, depression, and loneliness.

5. *"Show me the way I should go, for to you I entrust my life."* (Verse 8) **Ask God for wisdom!** Ask Him to show you the way you should go today! He will!

6. *"Teach me to do your will, . . . may your good Spirit lead me on level ground."* (Verse 10) **Invite the Holy Spirit to lead you, teach you, and empower you today!**

7. *"For your name's sake, LORD, preserve my life; in your righteousness, bring me out of trouble."* (Verse 11) **Remind God of His covenant. He will deliver you, because He swore He would.** (Hebrews 6:13)

He swore with His blood that He would keep His promises to you. Ask Him to deliver you completely out of the specific trouble you are in.

"Many are the afflictions of the righteous, BUT the Lord delivers him out of them all." (Psalm 34:19)

Remember, it's the entrance of His Word that brings light. Darkness has to flee when you turn the light on. Never forget that God loves you; He's with you; and He's on your side. When you believe that, everything is going to be alright!

A RESPONSE TO LONELINESS

Chapter Fourteen

Make this declaration every day for the next 30 days; and watch what will happen in your soul. And say it out-loud!

"I will greet this day with God's love in my heart! It is the greatest secret to fulfillment and success no matter what life brings. It calms every storm. When the enemy persecutes my soul, love comforts it. When I face darkness, love brings light. When my heart is overwhelmed, love will inspire and encourage it! When my heart is distressed, love will remind me of God's goodness over the years.

When I feel discouraged, love will lift my hands to the Lord, and fill my mouth with a song. I will worship Him this day with His love in my heart!

I will greet this day with God's love in my heart! When it feels like heaven is silent, love will remind me that God knows what I'm going through. He has a plan. And He will provide for my every need.

I will greet this day with God's love in my heart! Love will lead me. Love will direct me. Love will inspire me. Love will heal me. Love will fill me. Love will revive me.

I will greet this day with God's love in my heart! Love will deliver me from my enemies. It will protect me in times of storm. Because of God's love today, all those who seek to hurt me will be stopped, for love makes my shield of faith work!

I will love all that I come in contact with today. I will love the weak and make them strong. I will love the inspired and be inspired by them. I will love the empty, and help them be filled. I will love the filled, and they will overflow! I will love the broken and they will be healed.

I will greet this day with God's love in my heart, and it will quench all the fiery darts of the wicked one. I will confront everyone I face, with God's love. It will shine through my eyes, bring a smile to my face; and bring waves of peace through my voice. It will lower people's defenses and empower them to experience God's presence!

I will greet this day with God's love in my heart! Because He loves me, I will love myself. I will love others. And I will love life, no matter what I face! From this moment forward, fear and hate leave my body and my mind. Fear and hate leave my family and my home, in Jesus' Name!

Special Note: In each of my books, I desire to help lead people to the Lord—if they have never been born again, or are not certain of their salvation. Please use this for yourself or someone you know who may not know the Lord yet.

THE GIFT OF SALVATION

Your New Life Begins
with God's Love

"This is the kind of love we are talking about—not that we once upon a time loved God—but that He loved us and sent His Son as a sacrifice to clear away our sins and the damage they've done to our relationship with God."

—1 John 4:10b MSG

Christianity is not a religion. It is a relationship between God and you.

God loves you deeply and wants a personal relationship with you! The Love of Jesus Christ will sweep away your sin, loneliness, pain, and fear. He wants you to spend eternity in Heaven with Him, and the rest of your life on this earth walking with Him. If you would like to begin a new life—beyond your wildest dreams and be born again—pray the following prayer, and believe in your heart that God answers!

"Heavenly Father, I believe that Jesus Christ died on the cross for my sins and rose from the dead. His blood washes away my past, my sins; and prepares me for eternity. I receive Your forgiveness and accept Jesus as my Savior and Lord. From this day forward, I am Yours, in Jesus' Name. Amen!"

If you have prayed this prayer, we would love to hear from you. Please call us at 847-645-9700, or simply email us at prayer@changinglives.org.

AS YOU GO FORWARD

Next Steps

As a believer, I encourage you to step out in faith and live every day as if it were your first day living for God. I also encourage you to do the following three things:

1. Read your Bible. The Bible has the answer to every problem that you could ever face. As you read and study, know that you have the same promises that God gave Abraham, David, and all of the great men and women in the Bible. You will find out exactly who you are and what you mean to Him. You will find out that He will never leave you or forsake you! You will be filled with strength and wisdom.

2. Get planted in church. By now, you understand the power that comes from the church family. You don't need to go to church to get into heaven, but you **DO** need to become equipped to fulfill God's will for your life. In Luke 4:16, we find it was Jesus' custom to go to church every week. If the Son of God made it His custom, how much more should we?

3. *Tell Somebody.* One of the most rewarding things I have ever found in my life is the opportunity to share with others what God has done for me. You don't have to be a preacher. Just tell someone your simple story of God's love and plant the seed of the gospel in someone's life. You will be blessed, and so will they!

Well, what a journey you've just begun! And it is just that—a journey. Remember, the power of a new life is a process. It begins the moment you are born again, but it continues through our lives. We all face storms and trials, and we have an enemy, the devil, trying to stop our progress. But God has given us the tools and weapons to resist the enemy and be victorious in our journey. Build your life on these foundations and you will not fail!

"And the rain fell, and the floods came, and the winds blew and beat against that house; and yet it did not fall, for it had been founded on the rock." (Matthew 7:25)

Gregory Dickow Ministries &
Life Changers International Church Mission Statement

"Introducing people to the real Jesus;
empowering them to rise to their true worth
& purpose; and changing mind-sets
that change the world."

OTHER BOOKS AVAILABLE BY PASTOR GREGORY DICKOW

- Breaking the Power of Inferiority
- Fast From Wrong Thinking
- From the Inside Out
- How to Never be Hurt Again
- More Than Amazing Grace
- So Loved
- The Power to Change Today
- Thinking Forward
- Winning the Battle of the Mind

AUDIO SERIES AVAILABLE BY PASTOR GREGORY DICKOW

- Breaking the Power of Shame
- Command Your Day
- Fearless Living
- Healing the Father Fracture
- Identity
- Living in the State of Grace: Relocating to the Best Place on Earth
- Love Thyself
- Mastering Your Emotions
- Radical Acceptance
- The End of Religion
- The Holy Spirit, Our Healer
- Visions & Dreams

You can order these and many other life-changing materials by calling toll-free **1-888-438-5433**. For more information about Gregory Dickow Ministries, please visit **www.gregorydickow.com**.